SAINT PETERSBURG ...

ONCE UPON A TIME, THERE WAS AN ORPHAN GIRL WHO WAS AS BEAUTIFUL AS SHE WAS POOR. TO SURVIVE, SHE WOULD DO ALL THE THANKLESS JOBS HER NEIGHBOURS WOULD GIVE HER.

HER LIFE WAS AS ICY AS THE WATERS OF THE NEVA RIVER IN WINTER. SOMETIMES SHE WOULD PLAY IN THE STREET, ALONE, WITH A SMALL WOODEN SHIP WITH RED SAILS. ON A DAY FILLED WITH WIND AND SADNESS, SHE MET WITH AN OLD MAGICIAN WHO BECAME FOND OF HER ...

HE MADE HER A PREDICTION: BE PATIENT. ONE DAY, A SHIP WILL COME INTO THE HARBOUR. A THREE-MASTER WITH SAILS OF DEEP SCARLET ...

... ITS CAPTAIN WILL BE A RICH AND HANDSOME PRINCE FROM A LAND BEYOND THE SEAS. HE WILL MARRY YOU, AND YOU WILL FINALLY KNOW HAPPINESS.

ALYE PARUSA ... THE SCARLET SAILS. A WONDERFUL NOVEL KNOWN TO ALL RUSSIAN CHILDREN. THIS IS WHY, EVERY YEAR, WE CELEBRATE THE RETURN OF THAT SHIP, A SYMBOL OF HOPE AND PROSPERITY.

I PREFER THE MAGIC OF NUMBERS TO THAT OF FAIRY TALES.

HA! YOU AMERICANS WILL NEVER UNDERSTAND THE RUSSIAN SOUL. WE ALWAYS STAND FAST IN ADVERSITY.

IN FACT, I LOST A BILLION DOLLARS IN YOUR INVESTMENT FUND LAST YEAR.

MORE ACCURATELY 990,098,127 DOLLARS. YOU KNEW THE RULES. OUR KARISTA EQUITY FUND IS UNIQUE, AND ONLY OPEN TO WEALTHY AND DARING CLIENTS. UNFORTUNATELY, YOUR REFERENCE INDEX DIDN'T DROP AS YOU EXPECTED.

NE VAZHNO!* LET'S TALK ABOUT THE FUTURE INSTEAD. CHANGE THE DIRECTION, BUT NOT THE COURSE. I'M PUTTING ANOTHER BILLION IN THE SAME INDEX.

IN THAT CASE, PERHAPS I COULD SUGGEST LINX LABORATORIES INSTEAD? THEY AREN'T LISTED ON THE MARKET EITHER. THEY'RE ABOUT TO LAUNCH A NEW ANTI-OBESITY DRUG AND—

NO! THE SAME COMPANY!

*NO MATTER!

HMM! SUCH DOGGEDNESS! VERY WELL. YOU WILL WIRE THE AMOUNT TO OUR CLEARING HOUSE IN BERN, THROUGH THREE ACCOUNTS REGISTERED IN NAURU, PANAMA AND GUERNSEY. THE OPERATION WILL END ON DECEMBER 31 AT MIDNIGHT.

YOU WILL NOT BE ABLE TO ALTER EITHER THE INDEX OR ITS DIRECTION — UP OR DOWN. IF YOU GET IT RIGHT, YOU'LL ALWAYS HAVE THE OPTION TO DOUBLE YOUR STAKE UNTIL THE DAY BEFORE CLOSING.

AND IF I SCREW UP, I'LL LOSE MY BILLION — AND THE BEST THING I CAN DO THEN IS BLOW MY OWN BRAINS OUT.

WHY RISK SO MUCH? ...

ALAS, MY FRIEND! I AM ON THE VERGE OF RUIN, AND YOUR FUND IS THE ONLY ONE THAT OFFERS SUCH TREMENDOUS GAINS IN SO SHORT A TIME ...

VERY WELL, IF THAT IS YOUR CHOICE. OUR CLIENTS ARE FREE TO CHOOSE THEIR UNDERLYING INDEX AS THEY PLEASE.

'UNDERLYING ... INDEX'. SUCH COLD LANGUAGE ... TYPICAL OF A WESTERNER. ALL I SEE IS THE SCARLET OF THOSE SAILS. ALYE PARUSA, MY FRIEND. THE COLOUR OF WEALTH ...

THE COLOUR OF BLOOD ... MINE, AND LARGO WINCH'S.

4

YUCATAN, SIX
MONTHS LATER
...

YEP, THAT'S THE GUY
FROM THE PLANE WHO
OFFERED ME A JOB.*

NEVER MORE THAN
A WEEK IN THE SAME PLACE. IT
TOOK MY INVESTIGATORS FOREVER
TO PIN HIM DOWN ...

*SEE 20 SECONDS.

... THE UNPREDICTABLE IGOR MALIAKOV
... YOU'RE NOT GETTING AWAY THIS TIME.

YOU REALLY THINK HE WAS HOPING TO USE ME TO GET YOU
AND FINISH HIS DIRTY WORK AFTER HE FAILED IN LONDON?*

I DON'T THINK, SIMON. I KNOW.

BUT, YOU'D NEVER HAVE BEEN ABLE TO FIGURE IT OUT ALONE ... AND NEITHER
WOULD I! MEANWHILE, THAT SON OF A BITCH HAD ALL THE TIME HE NEEDED TO
ERASE THE LAST LEAD THAT COULD HAVE RESTARTED THE INVESTIGATION.

'LEAD'?! ... IS THAT HOW YOU TALK ABOUT THAT
CHICK NOW? SAIDEE? YOU WERE HEAD OVER HEELS
WITH HER.

SHE MANIPULATED ME.

SHE LOVED
YOU, LARG. SHE
SAVED YOUR
LIFE, TOO.

... BY DISREGARDING HER
OWN. I KNOW, SIMON. I KNOW
... AND I'M NOT GOING TO
REWRITE THAT STORY.

I AM, HOWEVER, EAGER
TO HEAR MALIAKOV'S!

5

¿QUÉ PASA?*

OK, SERGEI ... I'M COMING.

SECURITY CAUGHT AN INTRUDER.

JOIN ME IN 15 AND I'LL SHOW YOU WHOM I PREFER!

YOU PREFER YOUR GOONS' COMPANY TO OURS?!

*WHAT'S GOING ON?

SERGEI ?!

SERG— ??

SERGEI BANGED HIS HEAD ON A FLOWERPOT ...

TSK, TSK! READ IT! ?

SAIDEE ... FOUND DEAD LAST MONTH IN HER CELL. 'SUICIDE'. SHE WAS BEING HELD IN JAIL UNTIL HER TRIAL FOR HER PART IN A TERRORIST ATTACK AGAINST MY GROUP ... WHICH YOU ORDERED!

theguardian

headlines

FOUND DEAD

4

6

WINCH !?!

I HAVE THIS ONE UNANSWERED QUESTION THAT'S BEEN PLAGUING ME: WHY?

TO ... TO GET RID OF YOU ... BUT, I ... I WAS JUST FOLLOWING ORDERS.

AND TODAY, HERE IN MEXICO, ONCE AGAIN I FIND OUR PATHS *CROSSING*!!! GIVE ME THE NAME OF WHOEVER PUT A CONTRACT ON MY HEAD!

OR WHAT?

DOES THE PLAYBOY BILLIONAIRE INTEND TO TORTURE ME?

I WAS ONLY OBEYING ORDERS ...

IF I TALK, I'M A DEAD MAN.

WHOSE? TALK! ...

PROSHCHAY, MOYA LYUBOV.*

PAK

!!

AH, SHIT!

⑤

*GOODBYE, MY LOVE.

HIS NAME?

HHH ... DELO ... HHH ...

DELO ... REANHHHH ...

NO ... THAT'S IMPOSSIBLE! ...

DELOREAN. THAT'S THE CAR FROM *BACK TO THE FUTURE.*

HE WAS THE TARGET. A GOOD SNIPER WOULDN'T HAVE MISSED ME. LET'S SCRAM!

SO MUCH FOR OUR MEXICAN HOLIDAY.

WHAT MALIAKOV JUST GAVE US CHANGES EVERYTHING. THE STAKES ARE HIGH, SIMON. **VERY HIGH!**

MEANWHILE, IN NEW YORK CITY ...

DOW JONES
20,623

I'M SO BORED! ... THE MARKET'S ASLEEP! JESUS, HEAR MY PRAYER. GIMME A BULLISH* TREND ON BOEING AND I'LL GIVE YOU TEN PERCENT!

DON'T BE A CHEAPSKATE. GIVE HIM TWENTY PERCENT SO HE'LL BOOST MICROSOFT. I'VE GOT 12,000 SHARES TO UNLOAD.

*TERM REFERRING TO A RISING MARKET, IN REFERENCE TO A RUSHING BULL.

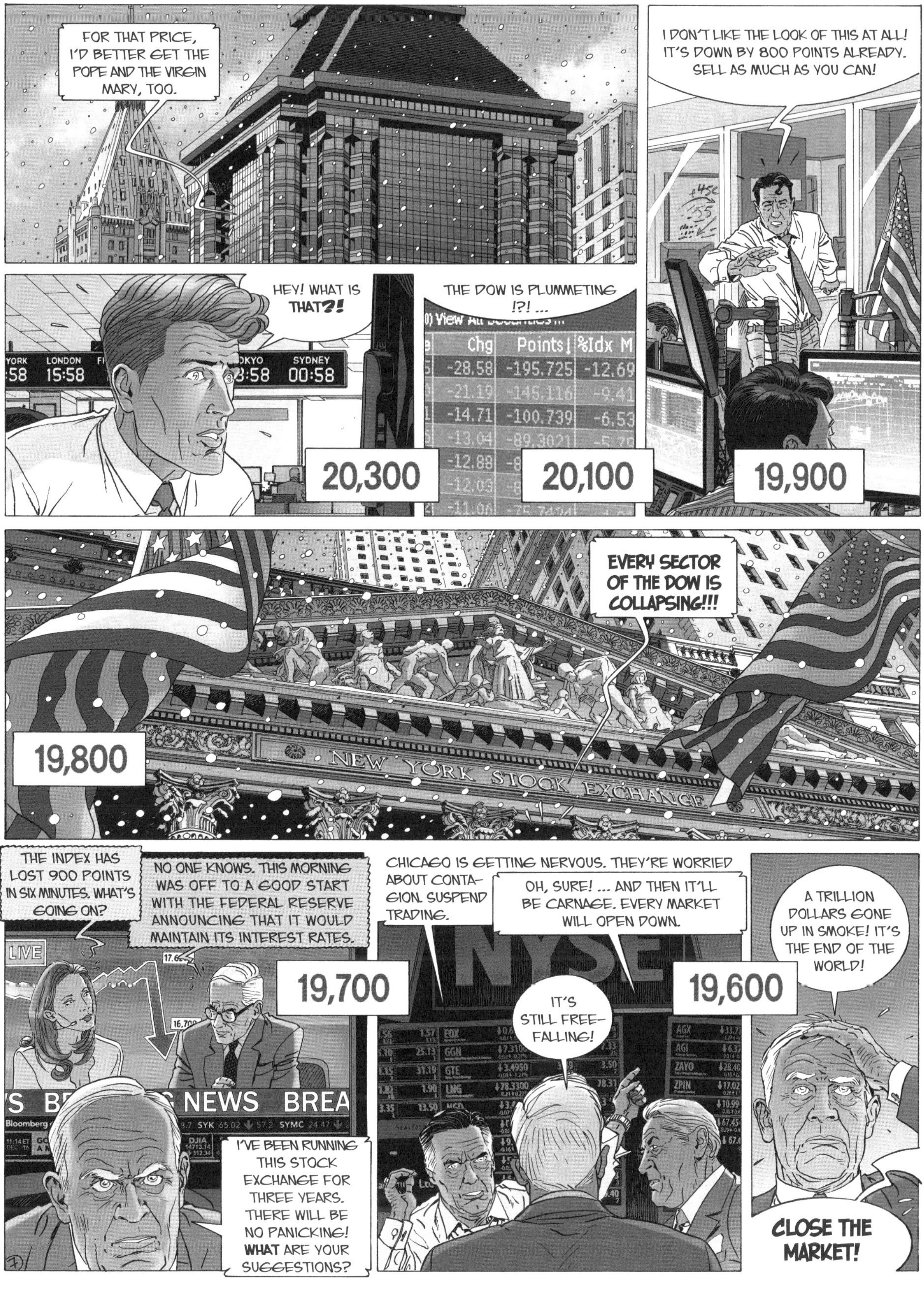

FOR THAT PRICE, I'D BETTER GET THE POPE AND THE VIRGIN MARY, TOO.
I DON'T LIKE THE LOOK OF THIS AT ALL! IT'S DOWN BY 800 POINTS ALREADY. SELL AS MUCH AS YOU CAN!
HEY! WHAT IS THAT?!
YORK LONDON TOKYO SYDNEY
15:58 00:58
20,300
THE DOW IS PLUMMETING !?! ...
Chg Points %Idx M
-28.58 -195.725 -12.69
-21.19 -145.116 -9.41
-14.71 -100.739 -6.53
-13.04 -89.3021
-12.88
-12.03
-11.06
20,100
19,900
EVERY SECTOR OF THE DOW IS COLLAPSING!!!
19,800
NEW YORK STOCK EXCHANGE
THE INDEX HAS LOST 900 POINTS IN SIX MINUTES. WHAT'S GOING ON?
NO ONE KNOWS. THIS MORNING WAS OFF TO A GOOD START WITH THE FEDERAL RESERVE ANNOUNCING THAT IT WOULD MAINTAIN ITS INTEREST RATES.
LIVE
BREAKING NEWS BREA
19,700
I'VE BEEN RUNNING THIS STOCK EXCHANGE FOR THREE YEARS. THERE WILL BE NO PANICKING! WHAT ARE YOUR SUGGESTIONS?
CHICAGO IS GETTING NERVOUS. THEY'RE WORRIED ABOUT CONTAGION. SUSPEND TRADING.
OH, SURE! ... AND THEN IT'LL BE CARNAGE. EVERY MARKET WILL OPEN DOWN.
NYSE
IT'S STILL FREE-FALLING!
19,600
A TRILLION DOLLARS GONE UP IN SMOKE! IT'S THE END OF THE WORLD!
CLOSE THE MARKET!

GET ME REGULATION ...

NO! WAIT!!!

19,500

THE *TITANIC* IS FLOATING BACK UP.

?!!

19,550

THE DOW IS IMPROVING. A SPECTACULAR RECOVERY, IN FACT.

TOO MUCH OF ONE, IF YOU ASK ME. I WOULDN'T BE SURPRISED IF THE SEC STARTS LOOKING INTO THIS SUSPICIOUS CRASH.

EXCLUSIVE 20,200 MARKE

Bloomberg HD 5 F 0.87 SYK

BUY BACK EVERYTHING YOU CAN. I WANT TO BE ABLE TO SMELL YOUR SWEAT ALL THE WAY FROM MY OFFICE!

20,300

THIS STINKS! FOR ALL WE KNOW, SOME CLEVER BASTARDS BOUGHT STOCK DIRT CHEAP DURING THE CRASH AND ARE OFFLOADING IT ON US AT XXL PRICES NOW.

NO WAY! NOBODY COULD HAVE FORESEEN THIS YO-YO EFFECT.

20,620

CHICAGO, AT THAT MOMENT ...

!!

WHERE TO, MISS?

GET OUT OF DOWNTOWN!

10

WASHINGTON, SECURITIES AND EXCHANGE COMMISSION, 1:00 PM ...

THE AMERICAN PEOPLE ARE SICK OF THOSE GREEDY TRADERS!

SEC: AMERICAN FEDERAL STOCK TRADING REGULATORY AGENCY.

WE CAME THIS CLOSE TO THE APOCALYPSE THIS MORNING IN NEW YORK — ONE TRILLION DOLLARS VANISHING, THEN REAPPEARING HALF AN HOUR LATER! THE PRESIDENT WANTS TO SEE HEADS ROLL.

THE TIME FOR COSY ARRANGEMENTS BETWEEN FRIENDS IS PAST. YOU'RE HEAD OF THE SEC — DO YOUR JOB. GOODBYE!

EVEN IMPORTANT ONES, MR SECRETARY?

A FINE BIT OF GRANDSTANDING! THAT GUY WAS AT THE HEAD OF THE COUNTRY'S THIRD LARGEST BANK DURING THE SUBPRIME CRISIS. BACK THEN HE WAS DROWNING IN TOXIC ASSETS AND BEGGING ME TO BAIL HIS ASS OUT.

A FINANCIAL CRISIS LESS THAN A YEAR AFTER HIS ELECTION — NO WONDER THE PRESIDENT'S ANGRY.

COLLEEN, WHAT HAVE YOU FOUND?

IT'S TOO EARLY FOR A DETAILED ANALYSIS, DIRECTOR. HOWEVER, IN TWO HOURS WE'VE MANAGED TO ZERO IN ON SOME SUSPICIOUS MARKET FLOWS. THIS IS WHERE FBI AGENT JOSS RANSON COMES IN.

THE FREEDOM ACT* ALLOWS US TO ACCESS ANY FINANCIAL MOVEMENT THAT ENDANGERS NATIONAL SECURITY. COLLEEN AND I TRACKED DOWN MASSIVE STOCK MARKET ORDERS PLACED BY SILVER TRADING, A BROKERAGE FIRM.

GOOD. MISS MCBRIDE, YOU HAVE CARTE BLANCHE TO BEGIN A PRELIMINARY INVESTIGATION. REPORT YOUR PROGRESS TO ME HOURLY.

MMM ... THE HUNT IS ON! CAN YOU SMELL THAT? THAT'S GIL VFP. TRADING BEING GRILLED!

JUST WAIT UNTIL I RELEASE THE HOUNDS. ONE OF MY EXES WORKS AT THE *FINANCIAL TIMES*' NEW YORK OFFICE.

*LAW ENACTED ON 2 JUNE 2015, THAT REPLACED THE PATRIOT ACT FOR THE PURPOSE OF PREVENTING TERRORIST ACTS.

CHICHEN ITZA, YUCATAN ...

I WILL CONCLUDE MY SPEECH AT THIS TALOS FORUM WITH A SUPERHERO STORY, AS IS FASHIONABLE THESE DAYS.

SUPER D-MAN ARRIVED ON EARTH AT THE END OF THE PRECEDING MILLENNIUM TO GIVE FINANCIAL MARKETS A BOOST. HIS SUPERPOWER? D FOR DERIVATIVES. CONTRACTS TO MITIGATE RISK IN ALL SORTS OF UNDERLYING ASSETS.

COMPANY STOCK, CURRENCY OR RAW MATERIAL FLUCTUATIONS, ETC ... THOSE DERIVATIVES WERE, FOR THE WORLD OF FINANCE, WHAT THE DISCOVERY OF FIRE WAS FOR HUMANITY. MANY AMONG YOU — NOT TO MENTION MYSELF — BECAME RICH THANKS TO D-MAN.

HE EVEN CREATED DERIVATIVES TO BACK THE ADJUSTABLE-RATE LOANS OF MODEST-INCOME AMERICAN FAMILIES — THE INFAMOUS MORTGAGE-BACKED SECURITIES, OR MBS, THAT FINANCIAL INSTITUTIONS FOUGHT OVER TO THE TUNE OF BILLIONS.

UNFORTUNATELY, IN 2007 THE RATES EXPLODED, HOMEOWNERS WERE UNABLE TO KEEP UP WITH REPAYMENTS, AND MBS PRICES COLLAPSED, CAUSING THE WORLDWIDE SUBPRIME CRISIS. FOUR TRILLION DOLLARS LOST.

$700,000 BILLION

$70,000 Bil.

THE LESSON HASN'T BEEN LEARNED. DERIVATIVES NOW REPRESENT TEN TIMES THE ENTIRE PLANET'S GDP — AND NEW ONES ARE CREATED EVERY WEEK WITH ZERO TRANSPARENCY.

Pr Lloyd Bancroft

DERIVATIVES ARE A MAJOR TOOL OF FINANCE, BUT THEIR UNCHECKED PROLIFERATION WILL LEAD TO AN EVEN WORSE CRISIS ... OH, I'M BEING ASKED TO STOP MY DOOMSDAY PREDICTIONS — IT'S TIME FOR THE COCKTAIL RECEPTION ...

YOUR PRESENCE HERE LENDS WEIGHT TO OUR WAR CHILDREN FOUNDATION, LARGO. THANK YOU FOR COMING. THE TALOS FORUM REMAINS THE MOST POWERFUL GLOBAL THINK TANK*, AND IT'S PACKED WITH GENEROUS PATRONS.

A PROMISE IS A PROMISE. BESIDES, IT GAVE ME A CHANCE TO TAKE CARE OF SOME BUSINESS NEARBY THIS MORNING.

*AN ORGANISATION DOING RESEARCH AND ADVOCACY ON PARTICULAR TOPICS.

MY SCHEDULE HAS CHANGED, THOUGH, CATHY. I'M FLYING TO CHICAGO JUST AFTER DINNER.

LARGO, AS ELUSIVE AS A GUST OF WIND ...

FREDDY AND THE COLIBRI ARE WAITING FOR ME AT THE CHICHEN ITZA AIRFIELD.

SORRY, I ...

DURAK!*

*IDIOT!

CHARMING. I'D MUCH RATHER GO SKINNY-DIPPING IN THE ARCTIC OCEAN THAN WADE HERE WITH ALL THESE SHARKS.

LEONID SOKOLIEV. RUSSIAN STEEL AND GAS TYCOON ...

AND HERE I WAS HOPING I COULD CONVINCE HIM TO SUPPORT OUR CAUSE ...

LET ME INTRODUCE YOU TO TALOS'S GENERAL SECRETARY, VIKTOR PALMINE. A MORE LIKEABLE OLIGARCH THAN SOKOLIEV — WHO'S HIS SWORN ENEMY.

LARGO WINCH! IT'S AN HONOUR!

THIS IS KSENIA NAIEVNA, MY DIRECTOR OF COMMUNICATIONS.

YOU'VE GOT YOUR WORK CUT OUT FOR YOU, COM-WISE. ON MY WAY FROM THE AIRFIELD I SAW HUNDREDS OF DEMONSTRATORS, ALL LOOKING A BIT TICKED OFF WITH YOUR FORUM.

POOR FOLK ... THOSE ANTI-GLOBALISTS HAVE SUCH A NARROW VIEW OF OUR WORLD.

MY GREATEST REGRET IS THAT I NEVER MANAGED TO CONVINCE YOUR LATE FATHER TO HAVE THE W GROUP LISTED ON THE STOCK EXCHANGE. WILL I BE LUCKIER WITH YOU?

PROFESSOR BANCROFT, I'M EVEN MORE STUBBORN THAN NERIO. YOU'VE HEARD WHAT HAPPENED THIS MORNING IN NEW YORK?

IT COULD HAVE BEEN ANYTHING. A BUG IN AUTOMATED TRADING SYSTEMS ... OR MAYBE 'FAT FINGERS' — SOME BRAINLESS TRADER TYPING BILLION INSTEAD OF MILLION.

COME WITH ME. LET ME INTRODUCE YOU TO SOME FRIENDS WHO WANT TO INVEST IN THE STOCK MARKET AND HELP WAR ORPHANS ... YES, YES, THEY'RE REAL!

'POOR FOLK' ... WAS THAT A REFERENCE TO DOSTOEVSKY'S FIRST NOVEL?

AN ORIGINAL OPENING, MR WINCH. ONE THAT TALLIES WITH YOUR REPUTATION.

THAT OF A COMMUNICATIONS PRO. THE ONLY BILLIONAIRE WHO GIVES LESSONS IN MORALITY AND RAKES IN THE PROFITS.

OH?! WHICH IS ... ?

WHAT ABOUT THE FACT THAT YOU ARE DOMICILED IN LIECHTENSTEIN? THE ONE AND ONLY SHAREHOLDER OF THE W GROUP? IS THAT HUMANISM? YOU HAVE YOUR WEAKNESSES, YOUR DARK SIDE, JUST LIKE EVERYONE ELSE.

DEAR ME, AND I DIDN'T BRING MY LAWYER ALONG. ISN'T THIS A RATHER HASTY JUDGEMENT?

HAHA! ARE YOU GOING TO TELL ME YOU HADN'T ALREADY PEGGED ME AS A RUSSIAN ESCORT? HIGH CLASS, I HOPE. YOU THOUGHT VIKTOR PUSHED ME INTO YOUR ARMS TO SPICE UP YOUR EVENING. SHOULD I CONTINUE ANALYSING YOU?

I DON'T LAY OFF MY EMPLOYEES TO INCREASE MY PROFIT MARGINS ... I DON'T RELOCATE MY FACTORIES ... I THINK THAT GIVES ME THE RIGHT TO VOICE MY OPINION.

I HAVE LITTLE TASTE FOR COUCHES, AT LEAST WITH SHRINKS. THOUGH IN YOUR COMPANY, IT WILL BE A PLEASURE.

COUCH *AND* PLEASURE. A REMARKABLE MACHO QUIP COMBINED WITH A PROPOSITION ... A PITY. I THOUGHT YOU WERE MORE SUBTLE THAN THAT.

SCHASTLIVA*, MR WINCH! I WILL SHINE IN MOSCOW WHEN I TELL THE STORY OF HOW I DIDN'T FALL FOR LARGO WINCH'S MACHO CHARM.

*GOODBYE, AND GOOD LUCK.

GOOD NIGHT ...

NICE!

PFF ... WE HATE MONEY, HERE!

D'YOU SELL THEM?

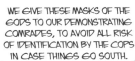

WE GIVE THESE MASKS OF THE GODS TO OUR DEMONSTRATING COMRADES, TO AVOID ALL RISK OF IDENTIFICATION BY THE COPS IN CASE THINGS GO SOUTH.

WASN'T IT THE MAYAN GODS WHO JUST LOVED A GOOD HUMAN SACRIFICE?

15

'WE HATE MONEY, HERE'??! ... THESE PEOPLE REALLY ARE A DANGER TO SOCIETY.

HIDE THE BODIES! I'LL CALL THE OTHER TEAMS.

WE HAVE SOMETHING IN COMMON, BUDDY ...

... WE DON'T BELONG IN THIS SETTING.

BZZ ...

BZZ ...

BZZ ...

BZZ ...

BZZ ...

BZZ ...

BZZ ...

BZZ ...

BZZ ...

?!?

fast FT

Telecoms — FT.com
https://www.ft.com

FINANCIAL TIMES

Today **DECEMBER 20, 2017**

Stock Market Crash

Trading branch of Winch Group, based in Chicago, could be involved in Dow Jones crash. Largo Winch under investigation (FBI and SEC).

Yesterday **DECEMBER 19, 2017**

SIGHTSEEING'S OVER, FREDDY. WE'RE LEAVING SOONER THAN PLANNED. PICK ME UP AT THE LODGE.

I DOUBT I CAN! IT'S A MESS HERE. THE POLICE HAVE BANNED FLIGHTS OVER THE AREA. THEY'RE SWAMPED WITH THE DEMONSTRATIONS.

I'LL MAKE MY WAY TO YOU, THEN ...

IT'S IMPOSSIBLE TO GET TO THE AIRFIELD. EVEN THE RUINS AND THE PYRAMID HAVE BEEN CLOSED TO TOURISTS. THE POLICE REPORT ANTI-GLOBALISTS EVERYWHERE WITHIN THE SECURITY PERIMETER.

WE ARE TRULY SORRY, MR WINCH.

IT'S ALL RIGHT. LEND MR WINCH MY FOUR-BY-FOUR.

IT'S ARMOURED, AND YOU CAN TAKE FOREST TRAILS.

?

HUH ... THANK YOU, MR ... SOKOLIEV, RIGHT?

YES.

I APOLOGISE FOR EARLIER. I HAD JUST LEARNED THAT THAT CROOK PALNINE HAD STOLEN YET ANOTHER CONTRACT OUT FROM UNDER ME. I SAW YOU TWO TALKING. NEVER DO BUSINESS WITH HIM.

I'LL REMEMBER THAT.

!!

¡¡MALDITOS PUERCOS!!*

WE ARE THE 99%

*DAMNED PIGS!!

17

¡LA PUTA MADRE! ¡CABRONES!*

WHAT DO WE DO?

NO PROVOCATIONS.

LARGO??

LARGO, ARE YOU LISTENING TO ME?

DON'T LET THEM INTIMIDATE YOU. YOU'RE THE HEIR.

I'VE BEEN HEARING THE SAME SONG FOR YEARS. IT GETS OLD.

'LET THEM HATE ME, SO THEY BUT FEAR ME.' YOU SHOULD READ SUETONIUS; IT'S ENLIGHTENING.

DID YOU HAVE TO RELOCATE THIS TOOL PLANT? YOU ONLY BOUGHT IT LAST YEAR.

WAGE COSTS ARE 70 PERCENT LOWER IN TAIWAN. I'VE COME TO TAKE RESPONSIBILITY FOR MY DECISION BEFORE THE UNIONS.

*OH, FOR FUCK'S SAKE! BASTARDS!

18

USUALLY IT'S MY DIRECTORS WHO HANDLE THIS SORT OF UNPLEASANTNESS, BUT I WANTED YOU TO FACE A REALITY THAT THEY'LL NEVER TEACH YOU ABOUT IN YOUR BUSINESS SCHOOL.

LESSON 1: A REAL BOSS DOESN'T SEEK HIS EMPLOYEES' LOVE. TO THESE PEOPLE, YOU WILL ALWAYS BE THE EXPLOITER AND THEY THE VICTIMS.

DID YOU HAVE TO PICK THE BENTLEY TO HUMILIATE THEM EVEN MORE?

LESSON 2: DON'T HIDE YOUR STATUS. THE BODY OF THIS CAR REPRESENTS AN IMPASSABLE BARRIER BETWEEN YOU AND THEM.

DO YOU KNOW WHAT I THINK OF YOUR BARRIER?! ...

?!

NO!!!

¿QUÉ COÑO?* I'M GONNA TEACH THEM SOME MANNERS!

NO-O-O-O, DON'T—

GET OUTTA HERE, YOU CLOWNS!

ANOTHER WORLD

ATTACK %

OCCUPY

WALLST NOW!

*WHAT THE HELL?

19

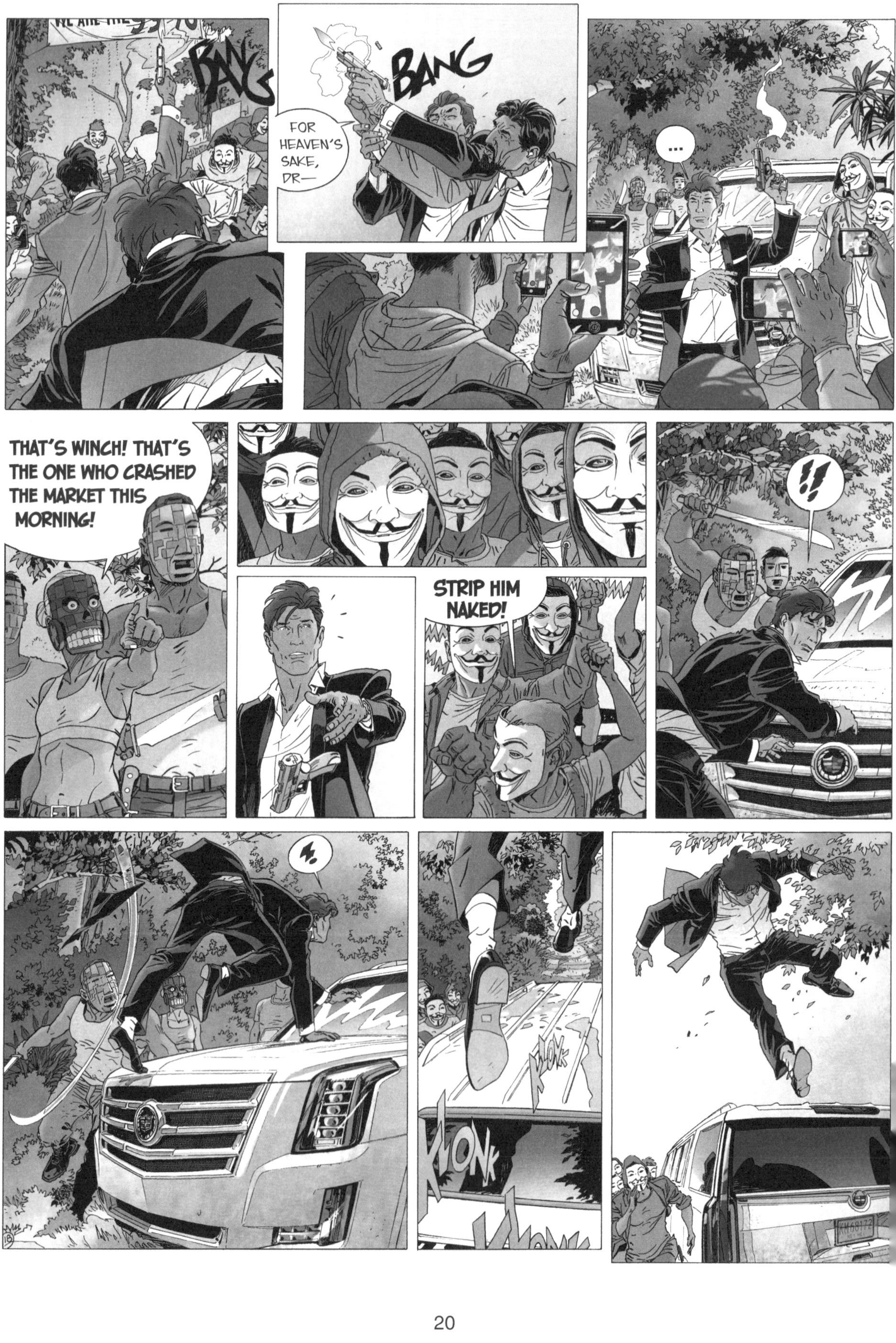
BANG
BANG
FOR HEAVEN'S SAKE, DR—
...
THAT'S WINCH! THAT'S THE ONE WHO CRASHED THE MARKET THIS MORNING!
STRIP HIM NAKED!
!!
!
KLONK
KLONK

THE 'FOX' HAS ESCAPED. WARN THE OTHERS THAT HE'S TRYING TO MAKE IT TO THE AIRFIELD. WE'RE JOINING YOU AT THE ARCHAEOLOGICAL SITE.

THE PYRAMID! I'M VERY CLOSE TO THE AIRFIELD NOW.

YOUR FOX IS HERE RIGHT ON TIME. CLOSING THE JAWS OF THE TRAP.

WHERE DID THEY COME FROM?

LARG, BUDDY, I THINK THIS TIME YOU'VE HAD IT! ...

21

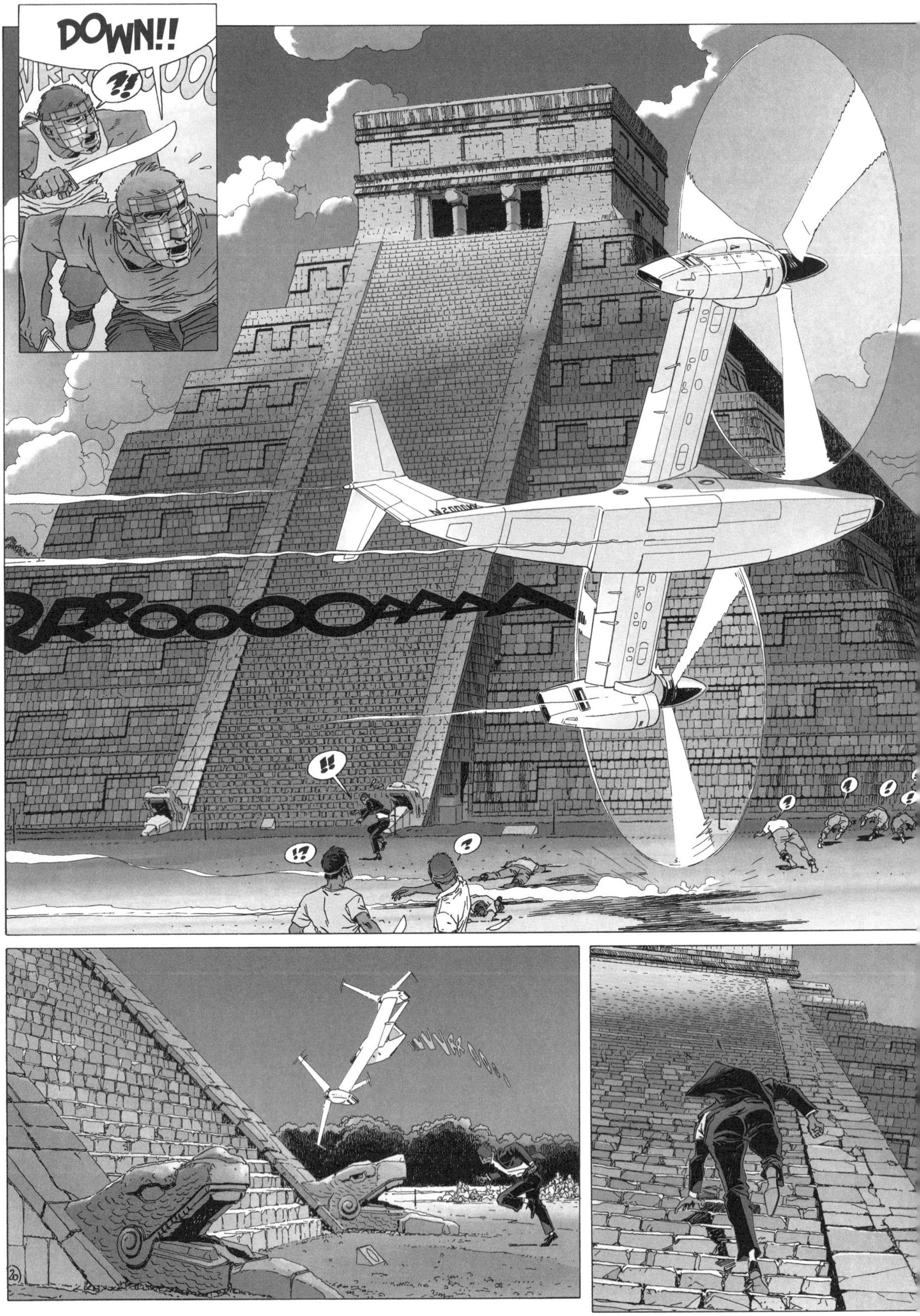
DOWN!!
?!
RRROOOOOMMM
!!
!?
?
!
!
!
!
WWVRR OOO...

WE'LL MEET AGAIN, MR WINCH, AND SOONER THAN YOU THINK ...

21

SAY 'THANK YOU, FREDDY, FOR GIVING ME A GPS TRACKER'.

I TURNED IT ON JUST IN TIME. THANKS, MOM.

WE'LL BE IN CHICAGO IN SIX HOURS.

I HAVE TO CALL DWIGHT COCHRANE.

OH! MR WINCH, AT LAST! I'M STILL MEETING WITH RUDI GESSNER.*

ARE THE ACCUSATIONS AGAINST SILVER TRADING JUSTIFIED?

GOOD EVENING, MR WINCH. A JUNIOR MARKET MANAGER AT SILVER BY THE NAME OF MARY STRICKER PLACED SOME ORDERS AND BYPASSED IN-HOUSE CONTROL. NET GAIN ON THE OPERATION: NINETY-EIGHT MILLION DOLLARS. THE GIRL'S GONE, AND THE MONEY VANISHED INTO OFFSHORE ACCOUNTS …

THE SEC AND THE FBI ARE COMING TO HEADQUARTERS TOMORROW MORNING. SHOULDN'T WE CANCEL THE BOARD MEETING?

NO WAY!

*HEAD OF THE W GROUP'S BANKING DIVISION.

THE ANNOUNCEMENT I HAVE TO MAKE IS TOO IMPORTANT TO THE FUTURE OF THE W GROUP.

… WHAT ABOUT SIMON?

OFF TO EUROPE. YOU'LL GO JOIN HIM RIGHT AFTER CHICAGO.

SLAVE DRIVER! IT'S A GOOD THING THEY INVENTED AUTOPILOT.

YOU'RE ALL GOING TO CONVINCE ME I'M A TERRIBLE PERSON …

!?

SO, SHOOTING AT POOR PEOPLE NOW, ARE WE?! IT'S ALREADY ALL OVER TWITTER AND FACEBOOK.

24

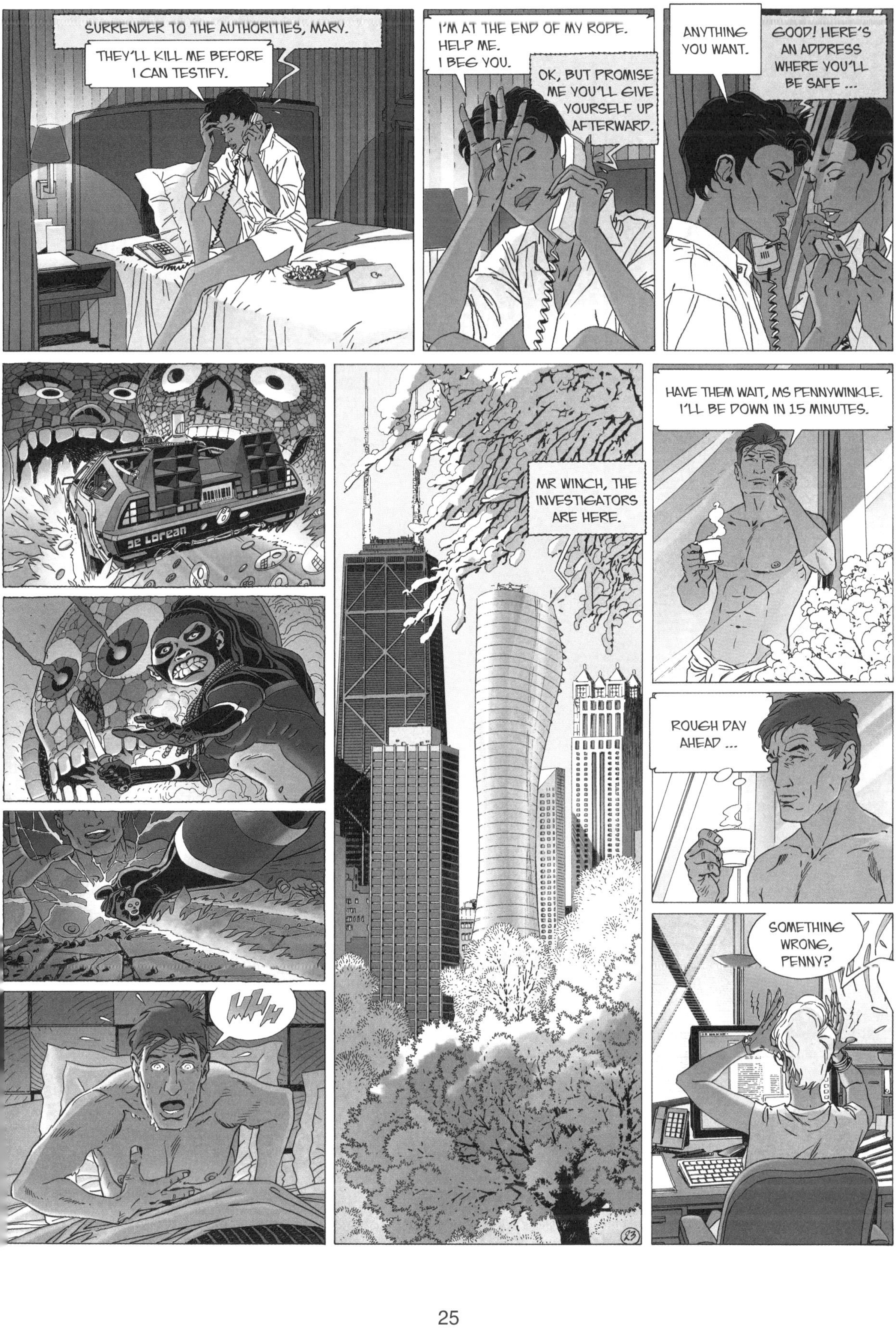

SURRENDER TO THE AUTHORITIES, MARY.
THEY'LL KILL ME BEFORE I CAN TESTIFY.
I'M AT THE END OF MY ROPE. HELP ME. I BEG YOU.
OK, BUT PROMISE ME YOU'LL GIVE YOURSELF UP AFTERWARD.
ANYTHING YOU WANT.
GOOD! HERE'S AN ADDRESS WHERE YOU'LL BE SAFE ...
De Lorean
MR WINCH, THE INVESTIGATORS ARE HERE.
HAVE THEM WAIT, MS PENNYWINKLE. I'LL BE DOWN IN 15 MINUTES.
ROUGH DAY AHEAD ...
SOMETHING WRONG, PENNY?

PFFF ... THE IRS! THEY'RE SLAPPING ME WITH AN UNJUSTIFIED ADJUSTMENT FOR 3,557 DOLLARS ... HAVE YOU EVER PAID TAXES, MR WINCH?

OF COURSE. MY SUBSIDIARIES DO SO IN THEIR RESPECTIVE COUNTRIES.

NO, I MEAN PERSONAL INCOME TAX. YOU KNOW, WHAT REGULAR PEOPLE HAVE TO DEAL WITH.

HOW TACTFUL OF YOU! THANK YOU FOR REMINDING ME THAT IT'S THANKS TO YOUR DEAR NERIO THAT I DON'T HAVE TO PAY TAXES HERE BECAUSE EVERYTHING PASSES THROUGH LIECHTENSTEIN.

YET ... 'THE OX IS SLOW, BUT THE EARTH IS PATIENT'. BURMESE PROVERB. BUT FOR NOW, I HAVE TO TACKLE THE SEC AND THE FBI. SEE YOU LATER, PENNY!

!?

OH, LARGO! I WAS DISCUSSING THE LEGAL RESPONSIBILITY OF OUR TRADER MARY STRICKER WITH MISS MCBRIDE OF THE SEC AND SPECIAL AGENT RANSON, FBI.

HER DISAPPEARANCE DOESN'T BODE WELL FOR YOU.

I DO HOPE SUCH A PROMISING TALENT WILL RESURFACE SOON — AND NOT AS A FLOATER IN LAKE MICHIGAN.

WHAT ARE YOU IMPLYING, EXACTLY?

YOU ACCUSING THAT WOMAN ... THAT'S FAIR ENOUGH. BUT MY SUPERIORS WARNED ME ABOUT THE TRAIL OF BODIES YOU TEND TO LEAVE BEHIND.

ARE WE DONE?

FOR TODAY, YES. OH, I ALMOST FORGOT. GENTLEMEN, YOU MAY NOT LEAVE THE COUNTRY UNTIL FURTHER NOTICE. HAVE A NICE DAY.

YOUR JUNIOR TRADER NEARLY MADE THE BIGGEST STOCK EXCHANGE IN THE WORLD GO KABLOOEY. SHE ALSO MADE JUST UNDER A HUNDRED MILLION DOLLARS IN HALF AN HOUR ALL OF IT BEHIND YOUR BACK.

WELL, MARILYN? WHAT ARE YOU DOING? DIDN'T YOU GET MY MAIL?

BUT ... I'M PREPARING THE ROOM FOR THE BOARD MEETING ...

IT'S NOT TAKING PLACE HERE, GIRL.

26

LUCERNE ..

CONSIDERING THE OUTRAGEOUS PRICES YOU ASK FOR YOUR SUITS, YOU COULD ...

... MAKE SURE THEY HAVE GOOD ZIPPERS.

IT LOOKS LIKE YOUR BOXER SHORTS ARE CAUGHT IN IT.

IF YOU MANAGE TO OPEN IT, I'M TAKING YOU OUT TO THE BEST RESTAURANT IN TOWN.

I'LL LET MY HUSBAND KNOW — HE'LL BE DELIGHTED TO JOIN US. I'M GOING TO GIVE IT A GOOD PULL. DON'T MOVE.

GOR-GEOUS, I— AYEEEEE!

OH ... SORRY.

UNBELIEV-ABLE!

Ermenegildo Zegna

FREDDY, MY GOOD MAN, TO THE BANK, NOW.

AND DO DRIVE CAREFULLY.

WOULD SIR LIKE ME TO PUNCH HIM IN HIS UGLY MUG?

WHAT NOW?

WE WAIT.

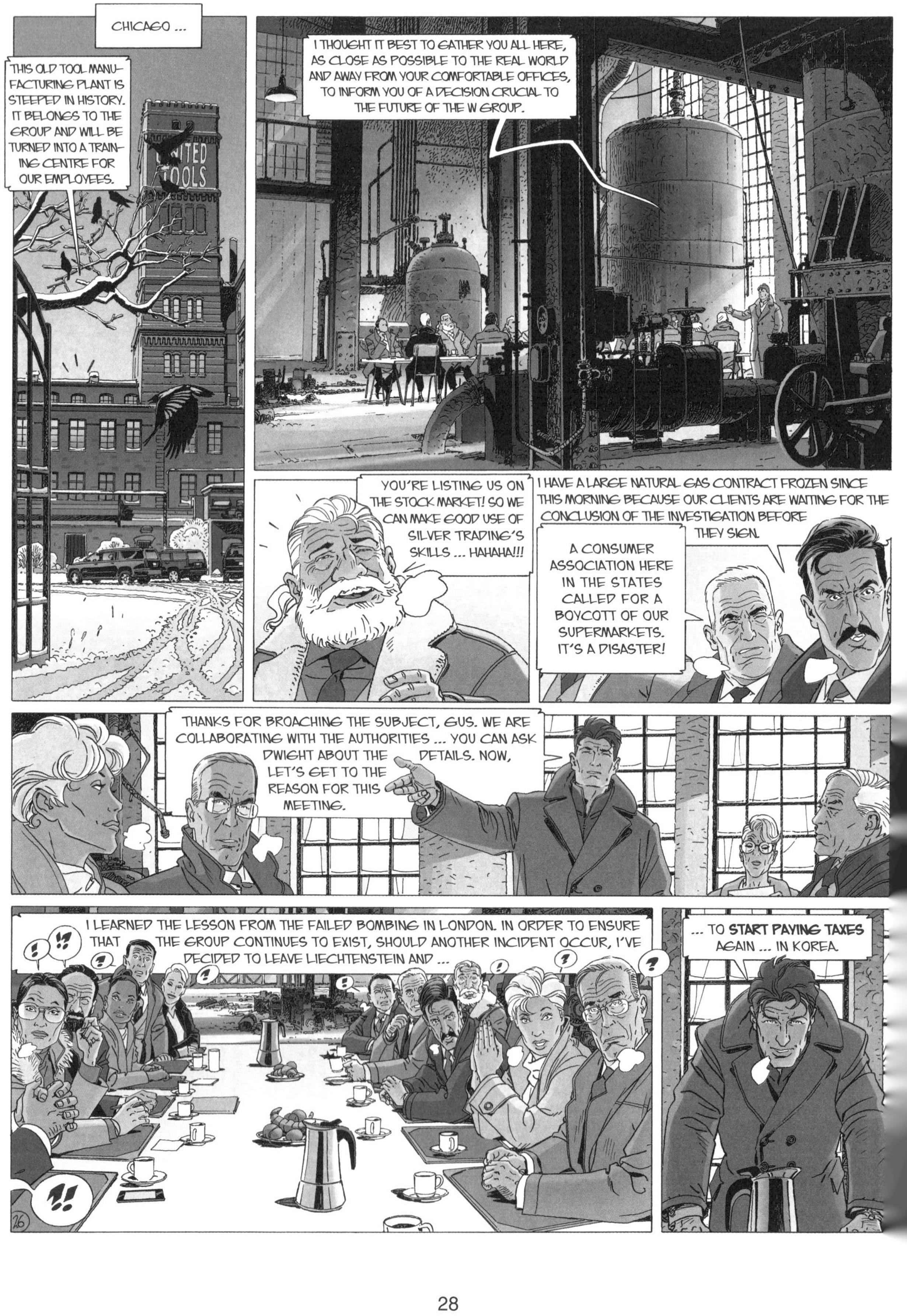
CHICAGO ...
THIS OLD TOOL MANUFACTURING PLANT IS STEEPED IN HISTORY. IT BELONGS TO THE GROUP AND WILL BE TURNED INTO A TRAINING CENTRE FOR OUR EMPLOYEES.
UNITED TOOLS
I THOUGHT IT BEST TO GATHER YOU ALL HERE, AS CLOSE AS POSSIBLE TO THE REAL WORLD AND AWAY FROM YOUR COMFORTABLE OFFICES, TO INFORM YOU OF A DECISION CRUCIAL TO THE FUTURE OF THE W GROUP.
YOU'RE LISTING US ON THE STOCK MARKET! SO WE CAN MAKE GOOD USE OF SILVER TRADING'S SKILLS ... HAHAHA!!!
I HAVE A LARGE NATURAL GAS CONTRACT FROZEN SINCE THIS MORNING BECAUSE OUR CLIENTS ARE WAITING FOR THE CONCLUSION OF THE INVESTIGATION BEFORE THEY SIGN.
A CONSUMER ASSOCIATION HERE IN THE STATES CALLED FOR A BOYCOTT OF OUR SUPERMARKETS. IT'S A DISASTER!
THANKS FOR BROACHING THE SUBJECT, GUS. WE ARE COLLABORATING WITH THE AUTHORITIES ... YOU CAN ASK DWIGHT ABOUT THE DETAILS. NOW, LET'S GET TO THE REASON FOR THIS MEETING.
I LEARNED THE LESSON FROM THE FAILED BOMBING IN LONDON. IN ORDER TO ENSURE THAT THE GROUP CONTINUES TO EXIST, SHOULD ANOTHER INCIDENT OCCUR, I'VE DECIDED TO LEAVE LIECHTENSTEIN AND ...
!
!?
?
!
!
?
!!
... TO **START PAYING TAXES** AGAIN ... IN KOREA.
26

NORTH KOREA.

I'M KIDDING.

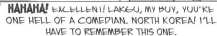

HAHAHA! EXCELLENT! LARGO, MY BOY, YOU'RE ONE HELL OF A COMEDIAN. NORTH KOREA! I'LL HAVE TO REMEMBER THIS ONE.

WELL, I'M ONLY HALF JOKING ... ONLY ABOUT NORTH KOREA.

HAVE YOU GONE MAD?!

WHAT?

WHAT? WHAT DID HE SAY? ...

HAVE YOU GONE MAD?!

YOUR YOUNG INTERN WAS EXTREMELY LUCKY, MR WINCH. HE'S FORTUNATE THAT THE GUARDS MOVED IN WHEN THEY DID.

YOUR BOSS ISN'T TOO HAPPY, IS HE?

YOU RECKLESS BOY! YOU WERE SUPPOSED TO REMAIN INCONSPICUOUS! NOT ONLY DID YOU NEARLY GET YOURSELF LYNCHED, BUT YOU'RE ALSO PUTTING THE FUTURE I PAIN- STAKINGLY BUILT FOR YOU IN JEOPARDY!

FOOL! YOU'D NEVER BE SAFE ANYWHERE, EVER, IF IT CAME OUT THAT YOU'RE MY SON.

ADOPTED ... ADOPTED SON.

I'LL RUSH THROUGH THE UNION MEETING AND WE'LL—

YOU DO THAT! I'M GOING ON DETOX THERAPY.

I'M GOING TO CLEAR MY BRAIN OF ALL YOUR LESSONS!

I'M RELOCATING — IT'S THE LATEST TREND!!!

GAZDA!?*

*BOSS!?

I'M FINE, VIRGIL. IT'S NOTHING. IT HAPPENS SOMETIMES.

I CATCH HIM?

NO. FOLLOW HIM AND MAKE SURE HE DOES TAKE THE FIRST FLIGHT FOR EUROPE. HE NEEDS TO FACE THE WORLD.

DA. DOBRO.*

*YES. VERY WELL.

WE'LL MEET AGAIN, LARGO. WHETHER YOU WANT TO OR NOT, YOU WILL BE MY HEIR.

TIMES ARE CHANGING ...

... THE PUBLIC CAN'T ABIDE SEEING THEIR OWN TAXES INCREASE WHILE MULTINATIONALS PAY ALMOST NOTHING.

AS YOU KNOW, THE W GROUP BELONGS TO ME THROUGH THE ZUKUNFT ANSTALT,* A HOLDING REGISTERED IN VADUZ. IT WAS CREATED BY NERIO IN ORDER TO TRANSFER OWNERSHIP OF THE GROUP TO ME WITHOUT PAYING DEATH DUTIES WHEN HE PASSED.

*A TYPE OF COMPANY SPECIFIC TO LIECHTENSTEIN, EXEMPT FROM TAXES ON ALL FINANCIAL TRANSACTIONS OUTSIDE THE COUNTRY. SEE THE HEIR.

THE DOCUMENTS CONFIRMING OWNERSHIP OF THE ZUKUNFT ANSTALT COME AS TEN PAPER DEEDS, IN MY NAME, ONE FOR EACH OF THE COMPANY'S TEN SHARES.

AS IT HAPPENS, AT THIS VERY MOMENT THE DEEDS ARE BEING WITHDRAWN FROM THE BANK AND TAKEN, UNDER ARMED ESCORT ...

... TO VADUZ, WHERE THEY WILL BE HANDED TO MY LEGAL REPRESENTATIVE, WHO IS ALREADY WAITING THERE. HE'LL PROCEED TO OFFICIALLY DISSOLVE THE ANSTALT — AN OBLIGATORY STEP TOWARDS THE CREATION OF A NEW ENTITY IN A DIFFERENT COUNTRY.

TEN SHEETS OF PAPER FOR A FIFTY-BILLION-DOLLAR GROUP ... THEY'D BETTER NOT FALL INTO THE WRONG HANDS.

QUITE SO! FOR SAFETY REASONS, THOSE TEN DEEDS ARE KEPT IN SWITZER-LAND, IN OUR LUCERNE BANK, THE STANDARD ANLAGE.

THEY'LL BE THERE IN THREE HOURS OVER THE BACK ROADS.

NOW FOR THE DAY'S REAL FUN: SAYING HI TO MY FORMER DAD-IN-LAW.*

*SEE COLD BLACK SEA AND RED HOT WRATH.

POOR OLD STROEGL. IT'S HIS WHOLE PROFESSIONAL PURPOSE THAT LEFT WITH THOSE DEEDS. SO, STAY COOL WITH HIM — BUT DON'T BE LONG!

DON'T WORRY! WE'LL TAKE THE AUTOBAHN — WE'LL BE IN VADUZ WELL BEFORE THEM.

YOU RIDICULED ME BEFORE THE ENTIRE BOARD! AND HOW MUCH IS YOUR LATEST SCHEME GOING TO COST US? ...

SHOULDN'T BE MUCH MORE THAN ...

...

WHY ... IT FALLS TO YOU TO FIND US THAT LAND OF MILK AND HONEY, MY DEAR DWIGHT. A GOOD SHEPHERD MUST SHEAR HIS FLOCK — NOT SKIN IT. REREAD SUETONIUS.

AND THE NAME OF THE HAPPY COUNTRY?

WHAT?

ONE BHHHHHHH ...

HHHHHH

I HAVE A PROFESSOR BAN-CROFT ON THE PHONE. HE HAS INFORMATION ON SILVER TRADING ...

I HAVE AN APPOINTMENT WITH LLOYD BANCROFT.

HE'S WAITING FOR YOU IN HIS OFFICE.

WELCOME. HERE, I MEDITATE ON THE CHAOTIC BEAUTY OF THE STOCK MARKET.

?!

DON'T BE SURPRISED. MY AMERICAN FATHER MET MY JAPANESE MOTHER IN YOKOHAMA. I AM A SON OF BOTH CULTURES — IN A WAY, I AM AN EMBODIMENT OF THE YIN AND YANG PRINCIPLE. OBSERVE THESE TWO DRAGONS.

THE MARKET IS THE ARENA FOR AN ENDLESS STRUGGLE BETWEEN THE BUYER DRAGON AND THE SELLER DRAGON. YIN AND YANG. THE PRICE OF A STOCK RISES OR FALLS WHEN ONE OF THE DRAGONS GAINS THE UPPER HAND OVER THE OTHER ONE. NEITHER WINS. THEY BOTH NEED EACH OTHER. OTHERWISE, THE MARKET WOULD NO LONGER EXIST.

GRANT ME A FEW MINUTES. IN THE 18TH CENTURY, SOME MERCHANTS IN TOKYO CAME UP WITH A METHOD TO PREDICT THE VAGARIES OF THE RICE MARKET, ONE BASED ON THE OPPOSITION OF YIN AND YANG. IT IS CALLED 'JAPANESE CANDLESTICKS'. THEY PREFERRED THE METAPHOR OF CANDLES, ARGUABLY MORE POETIC, TO THAT OF DRAGONS.

YOU DIDN'T BRING ME HERE FOR A LECTURE ON THE TAO. YOU CLAIM TO HAVE INFO ON SILVER TRADING.

??

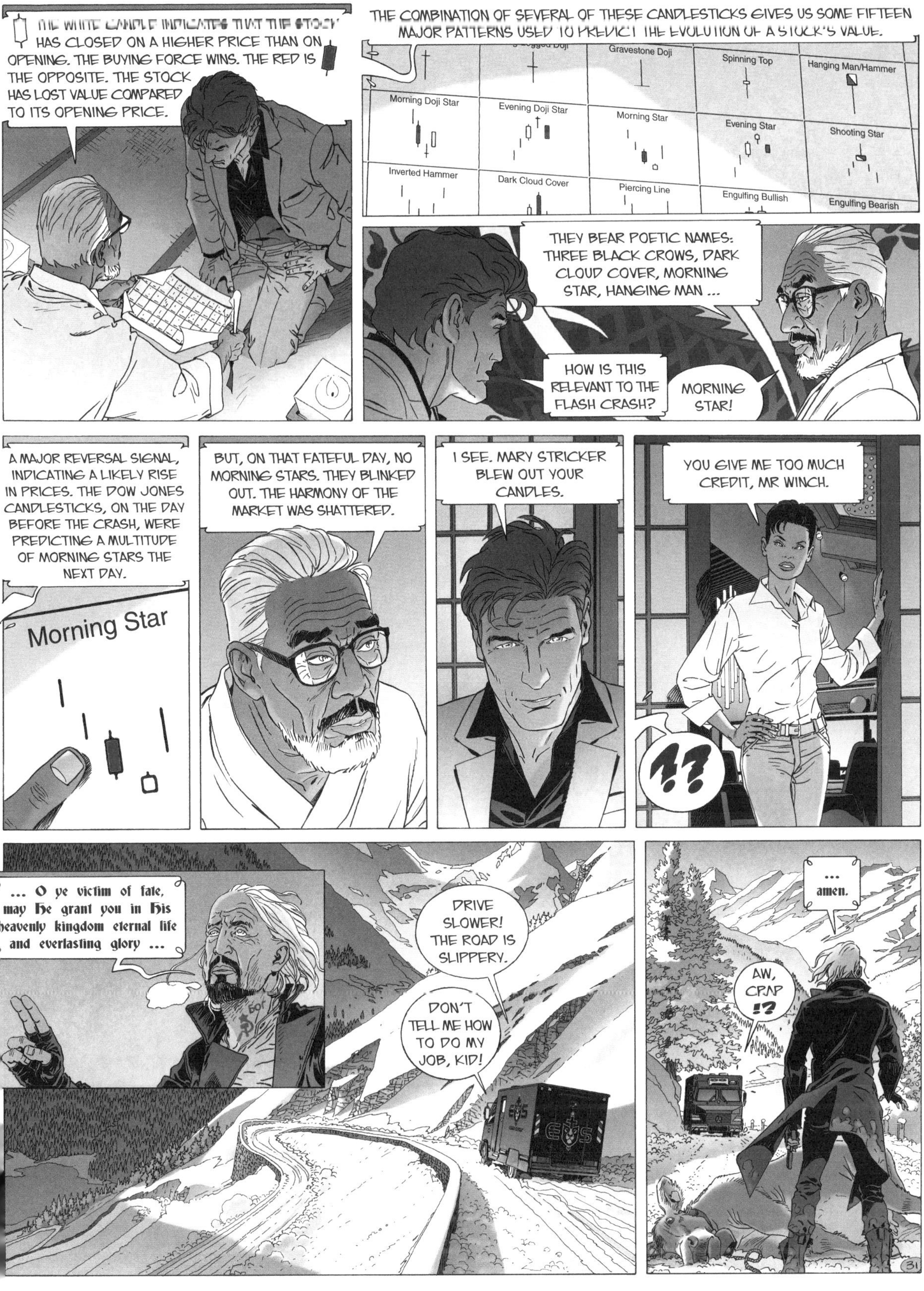
THE WHITE CANDLE INDICATES THAT THE STOCK HAS CLOSED ON A HIGHER PRICE THAN ON OPENING. THE BUYING FORCE WINS. THE RED IS THE OPPOSITE. THE STOCK HAS LOST VALUE COMPARED TO ITS OPENING PRICE.
THE COMBINATION OF SEVERAL OF THESE CANDLESTICKS GIVES US SOME FIFTEEN MAJOR PATTERNS USED TO PREDICT THE EVOLUTION OF A STOCK'S VALUE.
Gravestone Doji
Spinning Top
Hanging Man/Hammer
Morning Doji Star
Evening Doji Star
Morning Star
Evening Star
Shooting Star
Inverted Hammer
Dark Cloud Cover
Piercing Line
Engulfing Bullish
Engulfing Bearish
THEY BEAR POETIC NAMES: THREE BLACK CROWS, DARK CLOUD COVER, MORNING STAR, HANGING MAN ...
HOW IS THIS RELEVANT TO THE FLASH CRASH?
MORNING STAR!
A MAJOR REVERSAL SIGNAL, INDICATING A LIKELY RISE IN PRICES. THE DOW JONES CANDLESTICKS, ON THE DAY BEFORE THE CRASH, WERE PREDICTING A MULTITUDE OF MORNING STARS THE NEXT DAY.
Morning Star
BUT, ON THAT FATEFUL DAY, NO MORNING STARS. THEY BLINKED OUT. THE HARMONY OF THE MARKET WAS SHATTERED.
I SEE. MARY STRICKER BLEW OUT YOUR CANDLES.
YOU GIVE ME TOO MUCH CREDIT, MR WINCH.
!?
... O ye victim of fate, may He grant you in His heavenly kingdom eternal life and everlasting glory ...
DRIVE SLOWER! THE ROAD IS SLIPPERY.
DON'T TELL ME HOW TO DO MY JOB, KID!
... amen.
AW, CRAP !?
31

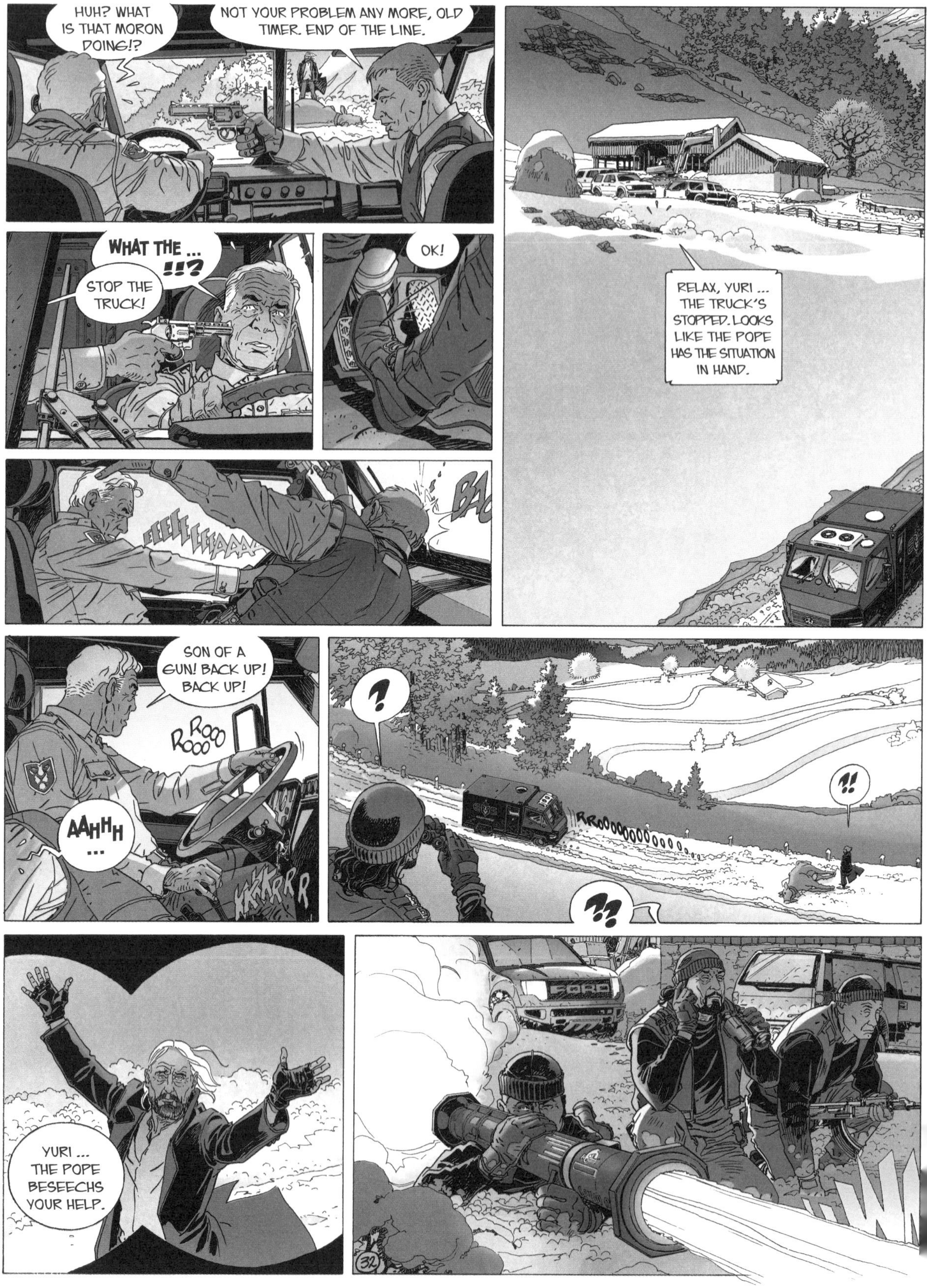
HUH? WHAT IS THAT MORON DOING!?
NOT YOUR PROBLEM ANY MORE, OLD TIMER. END OF THE LINE.
WHAT THE ... !!?
STOP THE TRUCK!
OK!
EEEEEEEEEEEEEAAAAA
RELAX, YURI ... THE TRUCK'S STOPPED. LOOKS LIKE THE POPE HAS THE SITUATION IN HAND.
SON OF A GUN! BACK UP! BACK UP!
ROOO ROOOO
AAHHH ...
KKKKRRR R
?
!!
RROOOOOOOOOOOOOO
?!?
YURI ... THE POPE BESEECHS YOUR HELP.

BY THE TRUMPETS OF JERICHO! ALEXEI, BRING THAT MECHANICAL MANURE SHOVEL DOWN HERE THIS INSTANT.

SHIT, SHIT, SHIT ...

SORRY, POPE. IT WAS THE DRIVER. HE—

LORD! THERE IS NO PERFECTION HERE ON EARTH. I SHOULD HAVE HIRED THE DRIVER.

YOU ARE A RANK AMATEUR. GO SWIM IN THE STYX.

O, SAVIOUR, RAISE YOUR ARM!

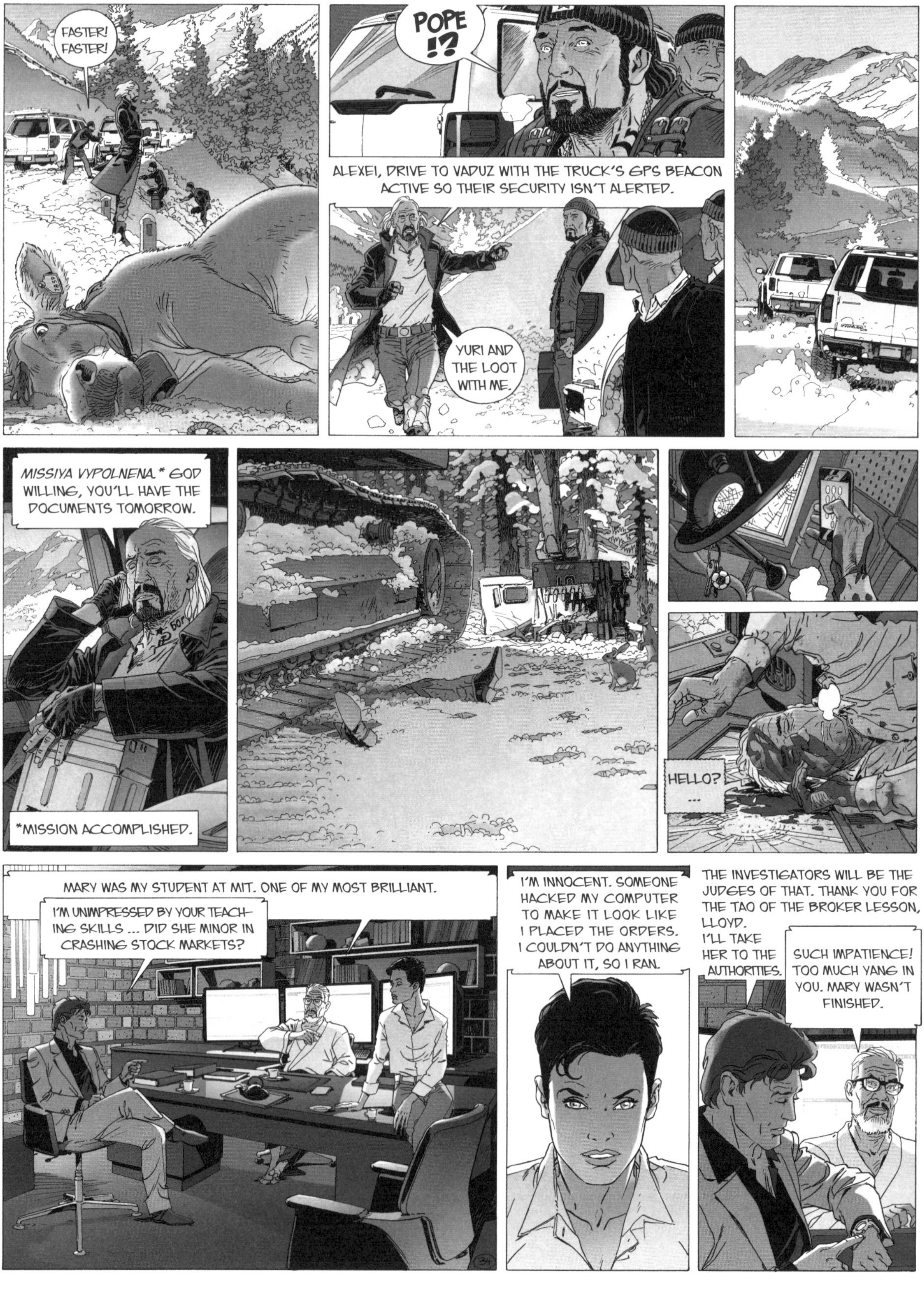
FASTER! FASTER!
POPE !?
ALEXEI, DRIVE TO VADUZ WITH THE TRUCK'S GPS BEACON ACTIVE SO THEIR SECURITY ISN'T ALERTED.
YURI AND THE LOOT WITH ME.
MISSIYA VYPOLNENA.* GOD WILLING, YOU'LL HAVE THE DOCUMENTS TOMORROW.
*MISSION ACCOMPLISHED.
HELLO? ...
MARY WAS MY STUDENT AT MIT. ONE OF MY MOST BRILLIANT.
I'M UNIMPRESSED BY YOUR TEACHING SKILLS ... DID SHE MINOR IN CRASHING STOCK MARKETS?
I'M INNOCENT. SOMEONE HACKED MY COMPUTER TO MAKE IT LOOK LIKE I PLACED THE ORDERS. I COULDN'T DO ANYTHING ABOUT IT, SO I RAN.
THE INVESTIGATORS WILL BE THE JUDGES OF THAT. THANK YOU FOR THE TAO OF THE BROKER LESSON, LLOYD.
I'LL TAKE HER TO THE AUTHORITIES.
SUCH IMPATIENCE! TOO MUCH YANG IN YOU. MARY WASN'T FINISHED.

I DID LOCATE THE ORIGIN OF THE HACK. IT CAME FROM THE SILVER TRADING HFT DATA CENTRE IN CHICAGO.

HFT?

HIGH FREQUENCY TRADING. THE PLACEMENT OF STOCK MARKET ORDERS BY COMPUTERS WITHOUT HUMAN INTERVENTION. SILVER TRADING HAS A CENTRE RIGHT HERE IN CHICAGO.

YOU'RE TELLING ME THAT A COMPUTER FRAMED YOU FOR ITS OWN EVIL DEEDS. IS THIS A JOKE?

NO. SOMEONE AT SILVER USED THE SYSTEM TO CAUSE THE CRASH.

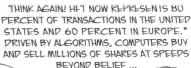

THINK AGAIN! HFT NOW REPRESENTS 80 PERCENT OF TRANSACTIONS IN THE UNITED STATES AND 60 PERCENT IN EUROPE.* DRIVEN BY ALGORITHMS, COMPUTERS BUY AND SELL MILLIONS OF SHARES AT SPEEDS BEYOND BELIEF ...

I'M HAVING A HARD TIME BELIEVING COMPUTERS CAN CAUSE A CRASH.

*IN VOLUME.

IN THE BLINK OF AN EYE, A MILLISECOND, AN HFT COMPUTER PLACES 8,000 ORDERS.

!!

AND WHEN THE COMPUTERS HICCUP, YOU GET A FLASH CRASH. ON MAY 6, 2010, THE DOW TOOK A TRILLION-DOLLAR DIVE BEFORE RECOVERING TEN MINUTES LATER. WHO CAUSED IT? AN HFT COMPANY THAT HAD PLACED MASSIVE ORDERS IN MERE MINUTES. THEIR COMPETITORS' COMPUTERS MISINTERPRETED THE INFORMATION, AND THE MARKET PANICKED.

WE CAME CLOSE TO THE END OF THE WORLD THAT DAY. TRADERS LOST AGAINST COMPUTERS. A FIRST IN STOCK MARKET HISTORY.

EVERY MICROSECOND, HUNDREDS OF HFT COMPANIES AROUND THE WORLD ARE ENGAGING IN INVISIBLE BATTLE. THEIR COMPUTERS ARE PROGRAMMED TO FOOL EACH OTHER BY PLACING MILLIONS OF BUY ORDERS ONLY TO IMMEDIATELY CANCEL THEM, SIMPLY TO INFLUENCE THE MARKET.

WHAT'S THE POINT?

THE QUICKEST ONE POCKETS THE MONEY. EXAMPLE: YOUR COMPUTER DETECTS AN ASSET THAT'S SELLING FOR $100 IN NEW YORK AND BUYING FOR $100.002 IN CHICAGO. IT PURCHASES 100,000 SHARES FROM THE FIRST EXCHANGE AND SELLS THEM, LIGHTNING-QUICK, ON THE SECOND. PROFIT: $0.002 PER UNIT — $200 TOTAL.

YOUR HFT COMPETITORS DETECTED YOUR MANOEUVRE, BUT TOO LATE. YOUR FIBRE-OPTIC CABLE BETWEEN CHICAGO AND NEW YORK GAVE YOU A TIME ADVANTAGE OF A HANDFUL OF MICROSECONDS. IN THE MEANTIME, THE PRICE DIFFERENCE HAS EVAPORATED.

TWO HUNDRED BUCKS? ... THAT'S PEANUTS.

IS IT? THAT'S $200 POCKETED IN A MICRO-FRACTION OF A SECOND! NOW, COUNT HOW MANY SUCH OPERATIONS CAN TAKE PLACE IN A SECOND, OR A MINUTE ... EVEN IF IT DOESN'T WORK EVERY TIME, AT THE END OF THE DAY THE PROFITS ARE IN THE MILLIONS. THAT'S A WHOLE LOT OF PEANUTS.

IF THE COMPUTERS KILL THE DRAGONS, MY CANDLES WILL GO OUT ...

YOU'LL BE CHARGED WITH ENDANGERING NATIONAL SECURITY. THE STOCK MARKET IS CONSIDERED A MAJOR STRATEGIC COMPONENT OF THE UNITED STATES. THE JUSTICE DEPARTMENT WILL DEMAND ADMINISTRATIVE SUPERVISION OF YOUR BANKING DIVISION, AND ...

... AND IN THE US IT WILL BLOCK THE CASH FLOWS OF THE GROUP COMPANIES CONTROLLED BY MY BANK ... THEREBY ASPHYXIATING THEM.

UNLESS WE FIND PROOF OF THE MANIPULATION. WE HAVE TO GO TO SILVER TRADING AND GAIN ACCESS TO THE HEART OF THE DATA CENTRE TO IDENTIFY THE CULPRIT.

EVEN IF YOUR HYPOTHESIS IS CORRECT, IT DOESN'T CHANGE ANYTHING IN TERMS OF MY RESPONSIBILITY.

ACTUALLY, IT MAKES IT EVEN WORSE. THE SEC WILL THINK ALONG THE SAME LINES AND FOLLOW THE SAME TRAIL. ACCUSING MARY WILL BE SEEN AS AN ATTEMPT TO HIDE YOUR HFT COMPANY'S RESPONSIBILITY.

THEN THERE'S NO TIME TO LOSE. IT SHOULDN'T BE TOO DIFFICULT — I OWN THE PLACE, AFTER ALL.

SAINT PETERSBURG ...

YOU SENT LARGO WINCH PACKING!

KSENIA, DARLING, YOU'RE CRAZY. YOU COULD HAVE SLEPT WITH HIM AND GOT YOURSELF HIRED.

PFF ...

HE'S YOUNGER, BETTER-LOOKING AND RICHER THAN YOUR PALNINE.

WE'RE DIFFERENT, SWEETIE. I NEVER MIX WORK AND FANTASIES ...

... ALSO, I DOUBT HE EVER HIRES HIS CONQUESTS.

BZZZ BZZZ

HOLD ON. I'M NOT ALONE ...

'MISSIYA WINCH' IS A GO ...

A PITY IT HAD TO BE HIM. THAT LARGO SEEMED LIKE A GOOD MAN. HAVE A GOOD EVENING.

BASTARDS, ON THE OTHER HAND, ALWAYS MAKE IT. AS YOU LEARNED THE HARD WAY.

CHICAGO ...

... LEAVE ME A MESSAGE ... BEEP ...

SIMON, IT'S LARGO! HOW'S OPERATION DELO-REAN GOING? CALL ME BACK.

WHY DID YOU CHOOSE TO BECOME A TRADER?

I WASN'T LUCKY ENOUGH TO HAVE A BILLIONAIRE FATHER, AND I LIKE MONEY ...

LIKE YOU, I IMAGINE ...

NOT REALLY.

MONEY IS A GOOD SERVANT BUT A LOUSY MASTER. I DISTRUST SPECULATION WITH THE HARM IT CAN DO.

OH?! SPEAKING OF DIS-TRUST ...

... YOU MIGHT WANT TO WORRY ABOUT YOUR E-REPUTATION. I LIKE YOU BETTER WITHOUT THE MOUSTACHE.

HUH?

HEIL!

?!

39

... IT'S YOUR TURN TO MAKE LARGO A VILLAIN: ADOLF LARGO, DARTH LARGO, JOKER LARGO ...

'BAD LARGO' IS TRENDING ON SOCIAL MEDIA ...

BAD LARGO? ... I'D PREFER MAD LARGO.

VADUZ
...

HOW WAS THE DRIVE FROM LUCERNE?

SMOOTH, PICTURESQUE, AND WONDER- FULLY BORING, SIR.

I MUST SAY I WAS SURPRISED ...

... WHEN MR WINCH CAME HERE LAST MONTH TO ARRANGE THE DISSOLUTION OF THE ZUKUNFT ANSTALT. TO LEAVE LIECHTENSTEIN AND REGISTER ELSEWHERE SO AS TO PAY TAXES AGAIN ... IN ALL MY DAYS AS A LAWYER, I'D NEVER SEEN THE LIKE!

DON'T BOTHER TRYING TO UNDER- STAND. HE GETS WEIRD IDEAS SOMETIMES. OUR PASSPORTS AND POWERS OF ATTORNEY.

PERFECT! AS FOR THE TEN DEEDS, THEY'LL ALLOW US TO PROCEED WITH THE TERMINATION. REGISTRATION WILL PROBABLY TAKE AROUND—

BZZZZ ...

THE CONVOY WAS ATTACKED.

LARGO WINCH, MAJORITY STOCKHOLDER OF SILVER TRADING. GET ME THE MANAGER RIGHT AWAY.

CHICAGO BOARD OF TRADE

MR WINCH! YOU SHOULD HAVE LET US KNOW IN ADVANCE!

TO WHAT DO WE OWE THE PLEASURE OF YOUR VISIT?

HI, PAUL. YOU'VE PUT ON WEIGHT AGAIN. A DESK JOB ISN'T GOOD FOR YOU.

MARY!?! HUH ... I THOUGHT THAT—

SHE'S WITH ME ...

... FOR A TOUR OF THE PREMISES — IN COMPLETE DISCRETION, THOUGH. CAN I COUNT ON YOU, MR WALKER?!

BUT, BUT, ABSOLUTELY, MR WINCH.

YOUR BOSS HAS JUST ARRIVED. DID YOU TAKE THE APPROPRIATE MEASURES, MR GESSNER?

OF COURSE. I BRIEFED THE DIRECTOR OF THE CENTRE.

GOOD. WAIT FOR NEW INSTRUCTIONS.

WELCOME TO THE RESEARCH DEPARTMENT. HERE, OUR SPECIALISTS DESIGN MARKET ANALYSIS ALGORITHMS.

EGGHEADS ARE REPLACING TRADERS ...

'JONAS' — OUR LORD AND MASTER YES, OF COURSE.

I'D LIKE TO SEE THE CENTRAL SERVER.

THE DATA CENTRE IS PROTECTED BY AN ELECTROMAGNETIC JAMMING SYSTEM. BEYOND THESE DOORS, CELL PHONES WILL NOT WORK.

WHY SET UP SHOP IN THIS OLD STOCK EXCHANGE BUILDING?

TO BE AS CLOSE AS WE CAN ...

... AND SHORTEN THE DATA'S TRAVEL DISTANCE. IN OTHER WORDS, TO SHAVE OFF TIME. TIME ISN'T JUST MONEY HERE — IT'S **PURE GOLD!**

BEEEP
IDENTIFYING

JONAS WELCOMES YOU, Mr WALKER

JONAS IS CONNECTED TO EVERY OTHER EXCHANGE IN THE WORLD BY FIBRE-OPTIC CABLE. THREE HUNDRED MILLION DOLLARS ... YOU MADE A WISE INVESTMENT.

I DO NOT SHARE YOUR ENTHUSIASM.

WE NEED TO BE ALONE SO I CAN GET INSIDE JONAS'S DATABASE. I DON'T WANT HIM UNDERFOOT.

HMM ...

I'M GOING TO CONTINUE THIS VISIT WITH MISS STRICKER. ONE LAST FAVOUR, PLEASE — COULD YOU CALL MR COCHRANE AT THE GROUP HEADQUARTERS AND LET HIM KNOW I'M HERE?

PAUL?

MR WINCH?

ABOVE ALL ...

OHH! ... DON'T WORRY. JONAS IS THE ONLY ONE WITH A GREAT MEMORY AROUND HERE.

40

42

JONAS, THE TRADER OF TOMORROW. IT MOVES AROUND TEN BILLION DOLLARS EVERY DAY.

IT'S FREEZING! ...

OF COURSE. IT'S SO POWERFUL THAT ITS TEMPERATURE RISES TO 160 DEGREES FAHRENHEIT. IT'S LIQUID-COOLED — COLD WATER IN PIPES RUNNING THROUGHOUT THE DATA CENTRE PREVENT IT FROM OVERHEATING.

OK. FIRST, FIND THE RIGHT ACCESS, THEN SNEAK INTO ITS BRAIN.

I HOPE THIS WON'T TAKE FOREVER. I WAS WAITING FOR A FRIEND TO CALL ME. HE'S GOT MY GROUP'S FUTURE IN HIS HANDS.

MAKE IT QUICK, COLLEEN! I HAVE A RECEPTION IN BALTIMORE, AND I SHOULD HAVE LEFT AN HOUR AGO ALREADY.

THE SECRETARY OF THE TREASURY WILL BE THERE.

WE HAVE SOMETHING, SIR. SOMETHING JUICY.

43

THAT TRADER WAS A FALSE LEAD. WE'VE RECEIVED AN ANONYMOUS EMAIL THAT POINTS US TOWARDS A HIGH-FREQUENCY TRADING CENTRE ALSO BELONGING TO SILVER TRADING.

SO, WINCH LIED TO US WHEN HE ACCUSED THAT WOMAN?

THAT'S MORE THAN LIKELY, SIR ...

TWO BIRDS, ONE STONE. I'VE BEEN WANTING TO CLEAN UP HFT FOR A LONG TIME. NICELY DONE, COLLEEN! YOU'LL BE THE WOMAN WHO BROUGHT DOWN LARGO WINCH!

JUST DOING MY JOB, SIR.

I HAVE THE UNPLEASANT FEELING I'M BURGLARISING MYSELF.

FINDING ANYTHING?

PATIENCE, BOSS ... CAN'T SEE A THING WITH THIS AQUARIUM LIGHTING. GIVE ME SOME LIGHT WITH YOUR CELL PHONE.

AND WOULD YOU LIKE A LATTE WITH THAT?

HOLD ON! I HAVE A TEXT MESSAGE. IT MUST HAVE COME IN JUST BEFORE WE ENTERED THE SERVER ROOM.

ARMOURED CAR ATTACKED!!! 1 DEAD

YOU'VE GOT A FUNNY EXPRESSION ALL OF A SUDDEN.

FUNNY ISN'T THE WORD THAT COMES TO MIND.

44

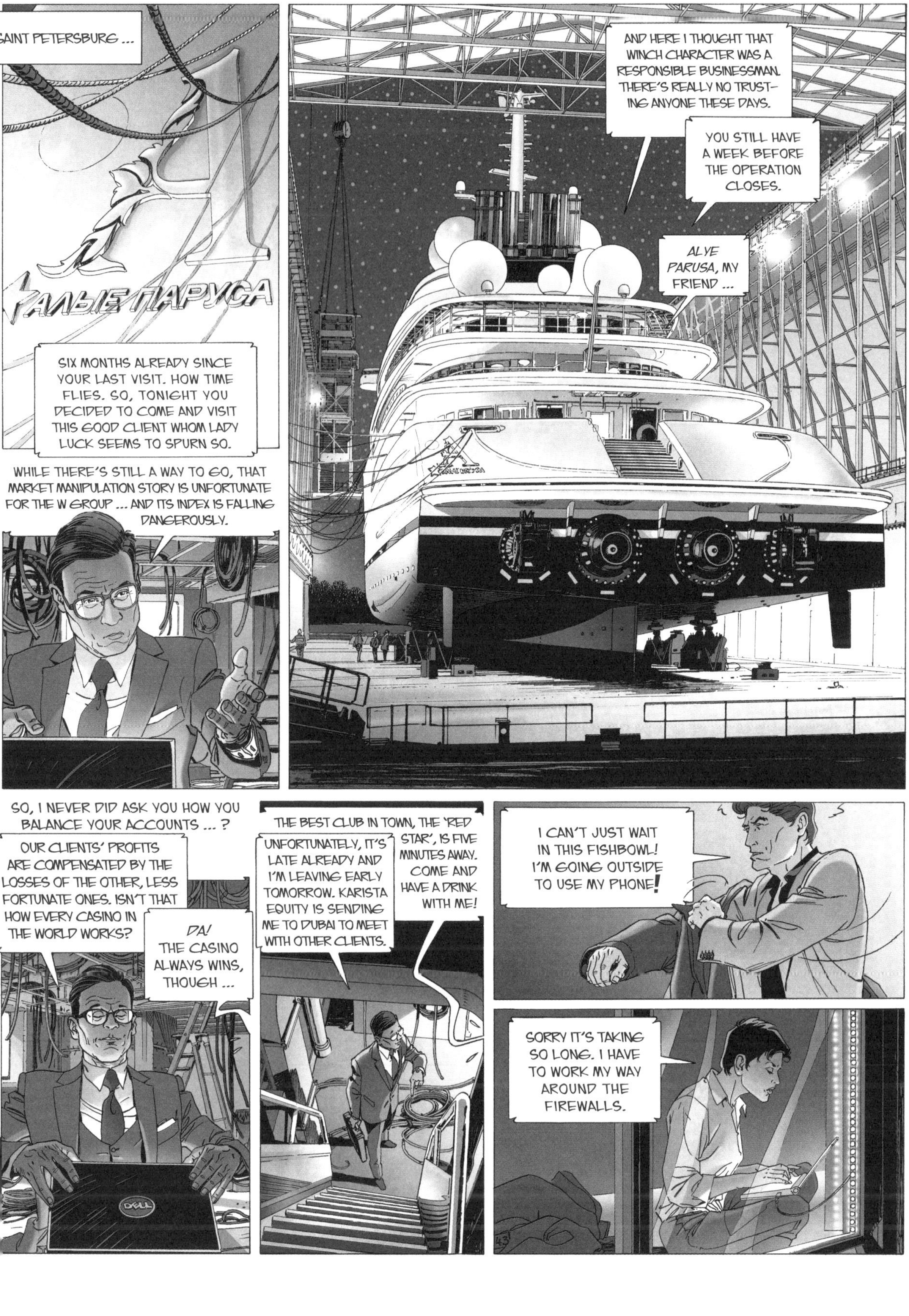
SAINT PETERSBURG ...
АЛЫЕ ПАРУСА
SIX MONTHS ALREADY SINCE YOUR LAST VISIT. HOW TIME FLIES. SO, TONIGHT YOU DECIDED TO COME AND VISIT THIS GOOD CLIENT WHOM LADY LUCK SEEMS TO SPURN SO.
AND HERE I THOUGHT THAT WINCH CHARACTER WAS A RESPONSIBLE BUSINESSMAN. THERE'S REALLY NO TRUSTING ANYONE THESE DAYS.
YOU STILL HAVE A WEEK BEFORE THE OPERATION CLOSES.
ALYE PARUSA, MY FRIEND ...
WHILE THERE'S STILL A WAY TO GO, THAT MARKET MANIPULATION STORY IS UNFORTUNATE FOR THE W GROUP ... AND ITS INDEX IS FALLING DANGEROUSLY.
SO, I NEVER DID ASK YOU HOW YOU BALANCE YOUR ACCOUNTS ... ?
OUR CLIENTS' PROFITS ARE COMPENSATED BY THE LOSSES OF THE OTHER, LESS FORTUNATE ONES. ISN'T THAT HOW EVERY CASINO IN THE WORLD WORKS?
DA! THE CASINO ALWAYS WINS, THOUGH ...
THE BEST CLUB IN TOWN, THE 'RED STAR', IS FIVE MINUTES AWAY. COME AND HAVE A DRINK WITH ME!
UNFORTUNATELY, IT'S LATE ALREADY AND I'M LEAVING EARLY TOMORROW. KARISTA EQUITY IS SENDING ME TO DUBAI TO MEET WITH OTHER CLIENTS.
I CAN'T JUST WAIT IN THIS FISHBOWL! I'M GOING OUTSIDE TO USE MY PHONE!
SORRY IT'S TAKING SO LONG. I HAVE TO WORK MY WAY AROUND THE FIREWALLS.

SPEAKING OF FIRE ... IT'S WARMER SUDDENLY. IS THAT NORMAL?

NO!?

WHAT'S HAPPENING?

COOLING SYSTEM BREAK- DOWN!!!

DON'T MOVE!

SHIT!

TO THINK THAT PALNINE AND SOKOLIEV USED TO BE LIKE BROTHERS.

WHY DID THEY BECOME ENEMIES?

SOKOLIEV TORPEDOED PALNINE'S ATTEMPT TO BUY THE LARGEST TELEPHONE OPERATOR IN THE COUNTRY. MY BOSS GOT HIS REVENGE BY SENDING SOKOLIEV'S WIFE PHOTOGRAPHS OF HIS WHORES ...

44

... IT TURNED INTO THE MOST EXPENSIVE DIVORCE SETTLEMENT IN RUSSIAN HISTORY.

HEY, LEONID! HOW HAVE YOU BEEN SINCE MEXICO? HAVE A DRINK WITH ME.

I GUARANTEE A TWO-BIT PLAYER LIKE YOU HAS NEVER TASTED ANYTHING LIKE IT — $90,000 A BOTTLE.

THANKS, BUT I ORDERED A CATHERINE THE GREAT AT $110,000.

DARYA, YOUR EX-WIFE — REMEMBER HER? ... I SOLD HER MY SMALL SAINT-TROPEZ YACHT FOR FOUR HUNDRED MILLION. I LOVE HER. SHE SPENDS YOUR DIVORCE MONEY LIKE A TRUE RUSSIAN WOMAN.

BE CAREFUL, VIKTOR. THERE ARE LINES ONE SHOULDN'T CROSS ...

DON'T THE COMPUTERS SHUT DOWN IF THEY OVERHEAT?

ONE BLOCK BREAKING DOWN TRANSLATES TO TRADING IN THE HUNDREDS OF MILLIONS OF DOLLARS GOING POOF. THE SECURITY SYSTEM AUTOMATICALLY ISOLATES NONREFRIGERATED UNITS BEFORE IT SHUTS DOWN EVERYTHING.

OH, KSENIA! THIS IS THE BEST CHAMPAGNE BATTLE OF THE YEAR. I BET YOU PALNINE IS GOING TO GO ONE BETTER AND ORDER THE $130,000 DIAMANTINA.

I NEVER BET ON THE STUPIDITY OF MEN. THE IMPOSSIBLE IS ALWAYS CERTAIN ...

NO NEED! ... WALKER MUST HAVE HEARD THE ALARM ...

BOM BOM

I ... I NEED AIR ...

ALMOST DONE ... FEEL ... FAINT ...

45

Éric Giacometti
&
Philippe Francq
2017

END OF THE EPISODE

COMING SOON
Scarlet Sails